IF FOUND

MW00878702

# Greater Than a Tourist Book Series
# Reviews from Readers

I think the series is wonderful and beneficial for tourists to get information before visiting the city.

-Seckin Zumbul, Izmir Turkey

I am a world traveler who has read many trip guides but this one really made a difference for me. I would call it a heartfelt creation of a local guide expert instead of just a guide.

-Susy, Isla Holbox, Mexico

New to the area like me, this is a must have!

 -Joe, Bloomington, USA

This is a good series that gets down to it when looking for things to do at your destination without having to read a novel for just a few ideas.

-Rachel, Monterey, USA

Good information to have to plan my trip to this destination.

-Pennie Farrell, Mexico


Great ideas for a port day.

-Mary Martin USA


Aptly titled, you won't just be a tourist after reading this book. You'll be greater than a tourist!

-Alan Warner, Grand Rapids, USA


Even though I only have three days to spend in San Miguel in an upcoming visit, I will use the author's suggestions to guide some of my time there. An easy read - with chapters named to guide me in directions I want to go.

-Robert Catapano, USA


Great insights from a local perspective! Useful information and a very good value!

-Sarah, USA


This series provides an in-depth experience through the eyes of a local. Reading these series will help you to travel the city in with confidence and it'll make your journey a unique one.

-Andrew Teoh, Ipoh, Malaysia

# GREATER THAN A TOURIST- NEW HAMPSHIRE USA

*50 Travel Tips from a Local*

Colleen Martin

Cover designed by: Ivana Stamenkovic
Cover Image: https://pixabay.com/en/new-hampshire-belknap-mills-river-69895/

CZYK Publishing Since 2011.

Greater Than a Tourist
Visit our website at www.GreaterThanaTourist.com

Lock Haven, PA
All rights reserved.
**ISBN:** 9781793860187

# >TOURIST

## 50 TRAVEL TIPS FROM A LOCAL

# BOOK DESCRIPTION

Are you excited about planning your next trip?

Do you want to try something new?

Would you like some guidance from a local?

If you answered yes to any of these questions, then this Greater Than a Tourist book is for you.

Greater Than a Tourist- New Hampshire, USA  by Colleen Martin offers the inside scoop on the Granite State.  Most travel books tell you how to travel like a tourist.  Although there is nothing wrong with that, as part of the Greater Than a Tourist series, this book will give you travel tips from someone who has lived at your next travel destination.

In these pages, you will discover advice that will help you throughout your stay.  This book will not tell you exact addresses or store hours but instead will give you excitement and knowledge from a local that you may not find in other smaller print travel books.

Travel like a local. Slow down, stay in one place, and get to know the people and the culture. By the time you finish this book, you will be eager and prepared to travel to your next destination.

# TABLE OF CONTENTS

# DEDICATION

This book is dedicated to my husband, and to my parents, who always believed in me.

# ABOUT THE AUTHOR

Colleen moved to New Hampshire for college almost a decade ago, and has never left. She is a freelance writer as well as a teacher. She loves to travel internationally, as well as going on daily adventures near her home. She enjoys wildlife-watching, outdoor education, and reading.

# HOW TO USE THIS BOOK

The Greater Than a Tourist book series was written by someone who has lived in an area for over three months. The goal of this book is to help travelers either dream or experience different locations by providing opinions from a local. The author has made suggestions based on their own experiences. Please do your own research before traveling to the area in case the suggested places are unavailable.

**Travel Advisories**: As a first step in planning any trip abroad, check the Travel Advisories for your intended destination.
https://travel.state.gov/content/travel/en/traveladvisories/traveladvisories.html

# FROM THE PUBLISHER

Traveling can be one of the most important parts of a person's life. The anticipation and memories that you have are some of the best. As a publisher of the Greater Than a Tourist book series, as well as the popular 50 Things to Know book series, we strive to help you learn about new places, spark your imagination, and inspire you. Wherever you are and whatever you do I wish you safe, fun, and inspiring travel.

Lisa Rusczyk Ed. D.
CZYK Publishing

# OUR STORY

Traveling is a passion of the "Greater than a Tourist" series creator. Lisa studied abroad in college, and for their honeymoon Lisa and her husband toured Europe. During her travels to Malta, an older man tried to give her some advice based on his own experience living on the island since he was a young boy. She was not sure if she should talk to the stranger but was interested in his advice. When traveling to some places she was wary to talk to locals because she was afraid that they weren't being genuine. Through her travels, Lisa learned how much locals had to share with tourists. Lisa created the "Greater Than a Tourist" book series to help connect people with locals. A topic that locals are very passionate about sharing.

WELCOME TO
> TOURIST

# INTRODUCTION

"Some old-fashioned things like fresh air and sunshine are hard to beat." – Laura Ingalls Wilder

One of the beautiful things about the Granite State is that you can experience so much variety in landscapes in just one state. In less than three hours you can drive from the craggy cliffs of the White Mountains to the beaches of the Atlantic Ocean. According to the USDA, roughly 88% of New Hampshire is covered in trees, making it the most forested state in America. Even much of the land area that isn't covered by trees is either mountainous terrain above the tree line, or lakes. It's an amazing place to experience the wilderness so close to civilization.

In addition to its natural beauty, New Hampshire has a wide variety of agricultural activities, as well as a few small cities and cultural centers, and of course winter sports. Most of the towns are relatively small, and many pride themselves on their small local businesses. Visiting some of these towns can sometimes give the impression of stepping back in time several decades, or even centuries. This New

England state might be small, but it has bountiful opportunities for all who visit.

This guide has been broken up into a few general sections to help you find what you're looking for. Some things overlap, but I think that's part of the beauty – one experience can you help appreciate multiple aspects of the state you're traveling to discover.

# NATURAL WONDERS

# 1. LAKE WINNIPESAUKEE

Two interpretations of the origin of the lake's name translate it as "The Smile of the Great Spirit" or "Beautiful Water in a High Place." Either name is fitting for the jewel of New Hampshire's aptly named Lakes Region. The largest lake in the state, this body of water and the surrounding towns offer recreation all year round. In the summer you can find people paddle-boarding, kayaking, and water-skiing. In the winter you'll see the lake dotted with ice-fishing cabins and sight-seers gazing across the icy beauty. In addition to water sports there's plenty of shopping and eating to do in the area. If you'd like to enjoy the lake but don't feel like getting wet, there are cruises many months of the year that offer tours and entertainment. My wedding and honeymoon took place in this beautiful area, and I highly recommend spending a weekend (or more!) enjoying a local B&B and the relaxing atmosphere by the lakes. There is a host of quaint lodgings in the area, many of which have some sort of waterfront access and their own boats, or small hiking trails attached.

## 2. MOUNT MAJOR

No matter the day of the year you're likely to find at least a few cars at the trailhead of Mt. Major. This hike is extremely popular, and for good reason. The parking lot is right off a main road, and though the walk up definitely constitutes a hike, it's not too strenuous and can be accomplished by people of a wide range of skill levels. I've seen small kids and eighty-year-olds, fit Siberian huskies and little French bulldogs all reach the summit. Besides being an accessible trail, the views at the top are absolutely stunning. There are sweeping panoramas of Lake Winnipesaukee, as well as the surrounding towns and forests. There are many wide boulders at the top that are a perfect spot for a picnic. The hike itself will probably only take you an hour or two.

The main trail and mountain can become a bit bogged down by crowds, especially on sunny days. If you're looking for a quieter hike to the same spectacular views, you can take the longer Brook Trail that winds around the back of the mountain, or you can turn down Jesus Valley Road (just south of the main parking lot) and hit a trailhead that offers the same natural beauty, with fewer tourists. For that one, you'll just park on the side of the road. All the trails are well-marked with colored signs.

# 3. LAKE SUNAPEE

Lake Sunapee is in the western part of the state. Away from the main Lakes Region, this lake is less well known but still a gem. It's surrounded by beautiful foliage and mountain. It was a very popular vacation destination in the Victorian era, and you can still see remnants of the railroad and steamboat industries. Rock n' roll fans may be excited to know that this is where the band Aerosmith hails from. Stephen Tyler reportedly still owns a house on the lake. Besides the history, the lake is a great place to enjoy summer activities such as swimming, stand up paddle boarding, or boating. If you feel like staying dry there are hikes of all grades in the surrounding woods. Kids might also want to visit the Mount Sunapee Adventure Park, or watch performances at the Barn Playhouse. In the evenings you can enjoy a lovely dinner cruise, or free concerts at the Ben Mere

Hotel's bandstand. In the neighboring town of a Sunapee Harbor there's a covered bridge and quaint shopping experiences, such as old-fashioned general stores and candy shops. For lodging you can stay in anything between budget motor inns and luxurious B & B's. You can also camp at either of the state parks, or any other local campground – some are primitive, while some have playgrounds and Wi-Fi.

# 4. WHITE MOUNTAIN HIKING AND CAMPING

Whole books have been written to guide adventurers through this area, but I'll try to do it justice in a page. The White Mountains are fierce but beautiful. They're wildly unpredictable and a joy to traverse. A mountain that offers a stunning vista one day might be enveloped in a torrential downpour and fog the next day (or the next hour). I've done hikes that take less than an hour each way. I've also done multi-day backpacking trips. One short hike that offered great views (and not a lot of climbing) was Mount Willard. It was less than two hours each way and there was plenty of room at the end of the trail to gaze out over the valley while enjoying some snacks.

A multi-day traverse I really liked went over the Presidentials (a group of the White Mountains that are named after various U.S. presidents). Trail markers were a little scarcer on this one, but we didn't have any problems finding our way. Going up in the higher peaks also offers a wider variety of terrain, including some little rock scrambles, and narrow winding paths through alpine forests, as well as paths through the more common northeastern forests.

One great way to enjoy an overnight trip is to use the AMC huts- it can be quite comforting to sleep in a solid wooden shelter at night, especially with such rapidly changing weather. It costs only a few dollars to sleep there, and you're guaranteed to meet some interesting people.

Taking a few minutes to research trip plans (there are many posted on hiking websites) can really go a long way so that you can get what you want out of the trip. The best advice I can give you is to bring layers, a map, and a camera, because you never know what you're going to find, but it's going to be wild and beautiful.

# 5. MT. WASHINGTON

Mt. Washington is the tallest peak in the Northeastern United States, and has been given the dubious honor of "Worst Weather in the World." It holds the record for the fastest wind gust ever observed by man at 231 mph. Don't let that stop you from visiting, though! Despite the extreme weather it sometimes experiences Mt. Washington is a beautiful place to visit. You can hike, ride the historic mountain cog-railway, or drive up the auto road to the 6,288 foot summit. It's not uncommon to see a car in New England sporting the sticker "This car climbed Mt. Washington." At the top of the mountain is an observatory and museum dedicated to weather research and science education. Researchers often spend time living at the observatory as they study the area's unique meteorology. They also always have at least one cat living up there for company! (Don't worry, it sleeps inside.) This mountain (when the weather is clear) offers awesome views of the surrounding area, and is of course a reward in its own right for simply having reached the top. The best time to scale this mountain is generally mid-May through early October. And no matter the time of year, bring extra equipment for snow.

# 6. THE FLUME

The Flume Gorge is a stunning nature walk in Franconia Notch State Park. The gorge runs along the base of Mount Liberty with walls of granite rising up to 90 feet above you. Over the course of two miles you'll experience mountain vistas, waterfalls, covered bridges, and a boardwalk through a deep natural chasm. You'll probably want to budget a couple of hours to enjoy the tour. You can buy tickets at the Visitor Center ticket office. The Visitor Center plays a free educational movie as well as providing gifts and food to purchase. The park is generally open May – October, but you'll have to check each year for the exact dates, and while they're open all day, the morning is definitely less crowded with less waiting time. Naturally, fall is an especially spectacular time to visit and view the foliage. But don't worry – the views will never disappoint, no matter the time of year.

# 7. LEAF-PEEPING

Leaf-peeping is a recreational activity in which people tour the countryside in the autumn, viewing the changing colors of leaves. People come from all over the world to experience the unparalleled foliage display that graces New Hampshire every year. Maple trees that produce the famous syrup also add beautiful swathes of red and orange to the tapestry of yellows, greens, and browns. In general leaf-peeping season runs from mid-September to mid-October. The absolute best weeks to visit are the first two weeks of October. New Hampshire's tourist website features a foliage tracker that to help you plan out what you might see and when. State parks and mountain roads offer great views, but there is equal pleasure in driving through back-country roads, enjoying the beauty of the woods in silence. Hiking is also a great way to experience the beauty of nature in a more intimate way. In the Lakes region, the Belknap Mountains are a moderate mountain range with a multitude of hikes that have great views. Monadnock Mountain, in the western part of the state, also offers spectacular views.

# 8. KANCAMANGUS HIGHWAY

Affectionately known as "The Kanc", this 34.5 mile drive is one of the best ways to experience New Hampshire's natural scenery. This American Scenic Byway cuts a path through the White Mountain National Forest, and offers breathtaking vistas of mountains, rivers, and waterfalls. At its highest you'll be at just over 2800 feet in elevation. It's a spectacular way to view foliage in the fall, but no matter the month or weather you are sure to be inspired by nature as you take in this scenic drive. In spring you can experience the bright green of newly leafed trees. In wintertime icicles and snowy views abound. Unlike on most other highways and byways, you cannot see manmade businesses and so this drive affords a unique natural experience. In addition to the scenery you'll likely to see a variety of wildlife, including eagles, deer, or bears. There are pullouts at several places along the drive in which you can stop to admire the views and take pictures. It's a great place to indulge in slow travel.

# 9. SCENIC RAILROADS

If you're looking for a unique, old-fashioned way to enjoy the scenery of NH, a train ride might be perfect for you. You can enjoy the Winnipesaukee Scenic Railroad (tours the Lakes Region), the Hobo Railroad (tours Franconia Notch in the White Mountains), or the Conway Scenic Railroad (tours the Mt. Washington Valley). Hobo Railroad also offers Santa Express rides during the holiday season. Depending on your budget and goals, these trains offer a spectrum of services, from a quick one-hour ride around Winnipesaukee to a five-hour ride through Crawford Notch with first-class dining experiences. Adults as well as children can enjoy the novelty of exploring the countryside in a classic, memorable way.

# 10. DIANA'S BATHS

Diana's Baths are a beautiful way to experience northern New Hampshire's natural scenery. A half mile hike from the parking lot brings you to a fascinating natural oasis fed from Big Attitash Mountain. Located in North Conway is a lovely mix of pools, cascades, and slides. There's only one major waterfall, which falls about twelve feet, and is structured in such a way that you can stand beneath the falling waters. Then its waters swirl and fall into a multitude of cascades over smooth granite boulders. The Baths are beautiful any time of year, and each season has its benefits. In the winter you can see beautiful icicles nestled in the snowy woods. In the spring, as snow melts, the currents can be quite strong but give the best show of waterfalls. The flow in summer is much more relaxed, making it the ideal time for visitors to wade in and. The Baths can be especially refreshing after a long hike.

# 11. MOOSE

With so much wilderness New Hampshire is a great state for wildlife watching. One of the most iconic animals is the moose. They occur in all counties of the state, though they are most common in the Great North Woods. NH State Park rangers will be happy to advise you on the best places to spot a moose, as these may change seasonally. A few perennial moose-sighting spots include roads north of Pittsburg, Lincoln, and Milan. Small ponds and clear-cuts in the woods are also good potential spots. In

Gotham NH, you can find moose tour guides that will very likely be able to bring you to an animal. The rut (their mating season) typically happens in early October, which gives wildlife watchers an opportunity for truly spectacular displays, but can also be more dangerous. Remember that although these animals can weigh over a ton, they are often difficult to see. It is important for the safety of yourself and the animals that you keep a safe distance away and use caution when searching for them. Never approach – enjoy the sight from a distance that doesn't stress them.

## 12. HAMPTON BEACH

I have to admit, Hampton Beach can get pretty "touristy," but it's for a good reason, and there are plenty of locals that enjoy the area. This whole area is full of summer activity – on any summer day you'll spot surfers, swimmers, and those who are simply out to enjoy some sunshine. The beach's sands are quite soft, which makes a nice change from the mostly rocky shores of New England. In the area you'll be able to find myriad restaurants, casinos, and shopping. The Boardwalk and beaches are often full of people playing and relaxing. Due to its popularity, parking can get tricky but if you're willing to get there during an off time (think weekdays especially) or walk a bit of distance from your car, you'll have no trouble finding a way. On specific days of the year, you can catch the Master Sand Sculpting Classic, Seafood Festival, Miss Hampton Beach Pageant, and other unique events.

# 13. SACO RIVER

This river in northern New Hampshire is shallow and wide, making it the perfect place for summer adventures. When it's warm you'll see groups of friends floating, paddling, or swimming down the river. It's relatively warm water but very refreshing, and can be a great place to kick back and relax. It can get a bit crowded around Conway, but there are plenty of places to put into the river and enjoy yourself.

# 14. STATE PARKS

With 93 parks covering over 4% of New Hampshire's area, there is something for everyone everywhere outdoors. Of course there are activities such as hiking and swimming, but in some parks you can try activities like archery, rock climbing, or horseback riding. The parks cost only a small fee (between $0-6 depending on age) and are really great recreational resources. Some are quite remote, but others are relatively close to population centers, making them great places to try your hand at camping.

## HISTORIC SITES

# 15. AMERICA'S STONEHENGE

No one knows what civilization built this group of rooms and walls, but at over 4,000 years old it is likely the oldest man-made construction in the United States. It has been determined that the site is an accurate astronomical calendar that can still be used to determine lunar and solar events. There are various inscriptions throughout the site written in ancient languages. In 2002 the vice-president Kelsey Stone added an alpaca farm that is now home to half a dozen alpacas that you can visit. A small visitor and gift shop supplement a self-guided tour that takes you through the mysterious history of these ruins. Located in Salem, a town that borders Massachusetts, the site is open every day of the year except for Thanksgiving and Christmas. There are special events on the equinoxes and solstices of the year.

# 16. MADAME SHERRI'S CASTLE

Touring the remains of a "castle" from the Roaring Twenties is definitely not your average woods-y experience. Madame Sherri originally made a name for herself designing Broadway costumes in New York, and at one point decided to build a place where she could entertain. While Madame Sherri lived in a smaller house in nearby Chesterfield, she built an enormous three-story structure with a large staircase outside the house. Eventually, her money ran out, and the house later succumbed to a fire, which destroyed all but some foundations and the staircase. You can now visit the ruins in the Madame Sherri Forest in Chesterfield, NH. Park in a small lot on the edge of the forest and cross a small footbridge for the Ann Stokes Loop, which runs about two miles through the forest. Soon you will enter into an open space filled with ruins. A sweeping stone staircase strewn with leaves arches to the sky but ends in mid-air. Scattered about nearby are columns and a large fireplace. You won't need much hiking gear, but definitely bring a camera. Whether this place is spooky or merely curious is up to you to decide.

# 17. STRAWBERRY BANKE

This history museum is alive! Instead of walking through dimly lit halls reading plaques, come learn about life in early New England by touring ten acres of a preserved historic site featuring tours and live re-enactors. The buildings are based on periods from colonial times through the mid-twentieth century, many of which are original restored buildings. The role players will largely remain in character as they educate you about what their lives were like in earlier centuries. Gardens, houses, and other living spaces have been preserved to provide an interactive learning experience about daily life in the old city of Portsmouth. Strawberry Banke also periodically host educational classes in hearth-cooking and basket making. This delightful learning site is open all months of the year, but a couple of events are my favorite. In May, the park hosts the Fairy House festival. These charming miniature houses are created by artists that range from kindergarten classes to extremely skilled professionals. You don't have to believe in fairies to enjoy the whimsy. In December, they hold a "Candlelight Stroll," in which visitors walk through houses showcasing 350 years of Christmas traditions and decorating.

# 18. FORT CONSTITUTION

The earliest fort on this site was built in 1632 by the British, and originally named Fort William and Mary. In 1791 it was repaired and renamed Fort Constitution. The fort has been employed in many wars since then, but is no longer active. It's free to visit and affords views of the Piscataqua River and Atlantic Ocean. Largely grassy, it's a great place for a stroll and maybe a picnic if the weather's nice.

# 19. CALEF'S COUNTRY STORE

Throughout New Hampshire's small towns you can find great little stores full of history. Calef's is one such gem. Upon entering the store, the sweet and savory mix of foods fills your nose as the old wooden floorboards creak beneath your feet. Open since 1869, this general store sells a variety of homemade and locally made treats and items. They sell their own molasses, honey, cheese, ginger, snaps, and jellies. The counters are lined with old-fashioned penny candies and scrumptious baked goods. I've also bought quite a few New Hampshire-themed gifts for family and friends over the years here. The staff has always been warm and pleasant. Stop in to stock up on locally made NH food and gifts, or maybe just to enjoy the homey atmosphere of their deli.

# 20. ISLES OF SHOALS

Take an island cruise out to a National Historic Site seven miles off the shores of New Hampshire. The border of Maine and New Hampshire actually cuts these nine islands in half (with four being property of NH). The long history of the islands includes John Smith's first footsteps in New England in 1614, as well as fishing and lighthouses. Island hotels were built here beginning in 1843 and you can still stay in the Oceanic Hotel on Star Island. The Shoals Marine Laboratory is based on Appledore Island, and in addition to hosting research for universities, they also run many educational programs for the public during the summer months and you can even book on a trip on UNH's marine research vessel.

# 21. PETERBOROUGH TOWN LIBRARY

This stop on the tour is for all book-lovers out there. Established in 1833, the Peterborough Town Library is the oldest tax-supported public library in the world. It celebrates the idea that access to knowledge should be owned and managed by the people of the community. Expanded twice in the past two centuries, its collection has grown from 100 books to over 43,000 today. In the back of the library you can sit in the original space, decorated by an old brick fireplace and portraits of the library's first staff. They also have a small makerspace for kids, and tons of activities free for the public.

# 22. ROBERT FROST FARM

Perhaps most famous for his 1916 poem "The Road Not Taken," Robert Frost lived in New Hampshire in the early 1900's, and his traditional New England farmhouse has been preserved as a monument to the acclaimed poet. Most of the poems in his first two books were written at this site. Frost reportedly said, "There was something about the experience at Derry which stayed in my mind, and was tapped for poetry in the years that came after." Touring this site will give you some insight into the lifestyle that Frost experienced and attributed many poems to. In addition to being a National Historic Landmark, the site offers tours, displays, and a nature/poetry trail. The poetry trail features poems outside along a stone wall, so that you can experience what they describe as you read. The staff is very knowledgeable and enthusiastic. There are also seasonal poetry readings, literary talks, and a nationally-acclaimed poetry conference.

# 23. COVERED BRIDGES

Few things say "quaint New England" like covered bridges. There's a certain charm to these old wooden structures, usually found on quiet back roads nestled in the woods. These 19th-century architectural gems are fun to photograph throughout all seasons of the year. The most famous might be the Cornish-Windsor Bridge – the longest wooden covered bridge in the United States and the longest two-span covered bridge in the world. Listed on the National Register of Historic Places, this bridge crossed between Cornish, NH and Windsor, VT (no surprises there). There are dozens of other bridges throughout the roads of New Hampshire, and they make for great sight-seeing any time of the year. A few dedicated people have assembled a map of all the covered bridges in the state, which you can find online. Scenic driving tours are one way to view the bridges, but if you can find one nearby it can be really fun to walk along the bridges, imagining yourself as one of those people that walked along those bridges for a hundred years.

# 24. MOUNT WASHINGTON RESORT

This historic hotel was built in 1902, and no expense was spared in its glorious architecture. When you walk these halls you walk the same path of many celebrities and U.S. presidents. Built in the same style as luxury liners such as the Titanic, walking through the halls and meeting rooms of this resort are an experience in themselves. And after you've feasted your eyes on the architecture, prepare to marvel at the spectacular views of the surrounding mountains afforded by the enormous windows throughout the hotel. In the lower level, you can visit The Cave – a stone-walled bar and lounge that was once a speakeasy. They feature live entertainment in a unique atmosphere. They also have an outdoor pool, which might be common for many hotels, but this one is heated in the winter! If you're feeling bold, you can run through the sub-freezing temperatures to the steamy pool outside. But don't worry – they serve plenty of hot chocolate inside. This resort is also closely linked to nearby Bretton Woods ski resort, and has its own cross-country ski trails and sleigh rides.

# 25. CASTLE IN THE CLOUDS

This unique place offers a lovely mix of history and natural scenery. Located in Moultonborough, the Castle in the Clouds property includes an Arts-and-Crafts style mansion that visitors can walk through, as well a few thousand acres of woods, trails, and ponds. You can take a guided pony tour, enjoy art at the Carriage House, or visit the gardens and fountains. Spring is an especially enchanting time of year to visit. And on a clear day, you'll have beautiful views of the surrounding Lakes Region. This is a great family activity, since adults can appreciate the history of the place while children can toss food to fish in the pond or run on many miles of paths, and all can enjoy the gorgeous scenery, and maybe even some ice cream.

# FOOD AND AGRICULTURE

## 26. FARMING AND THE LOCAL FOOD MOVEMENT

You might not be a farmer, but that shouldn't stop you from participating in a lively agricultural tradition that goes back centuries. The farm-to-table movement, as well as small farms, is strongly supported in New England. Most towns will host a farmer's market between the months of May-October. Visiting farm stands and farmer's markets can be a great way to connect with people and learn about where your food comes from. Perusing the available products can also help you learn a little more about the area. In particular, Stonewall Farm in Keene will give you a great hands-on experience of life on an old-fashioned farm, and give you a greater appreciation for everything that goes into growing great food.

# 27. HERMIT WOODS WINERY

There are many wineries in New Hampshire –
there's even a New Hampshire Wine & Cheese trail.
But one really unique winery I love is in Meredith.
The owner of this unique artisan winery is committed
to crafting wines only from plants that can grow in
the local climate. They are also committed to growing
their fruits using Best Management Practices. Tours
and tastings are a really fun and educational
experience. My personal favorite was their
wildflower honey-based wine, which truly tasted like
summer in a glass. If you're lucky, you also might
spot Pinot and Noir, two black cats the winery
adopted after a benefit for the local animal shelter.

# 28. SUGAR ON SNOW

This winter delight combines two of the things that
New England is most famous for – maple syrup and
snow! You might be invited to a "Sugar on Snow"
party, but you can also make your own at home.
Maple syrup is simply boiled, and then poured on
snow (either outside, or in snow you kept in your
freezer). At the right temperature, it will harden to
form a delightful taffy-like candy.

# 29. MAPLE

The maple syrup production season might be short, but this sweet concoction is a source of Yankee pride all year round. It's completely different from artificial syrup. I remember when I was young that finding maple foods was a rare treat. When I moved to New Hampshire I remember being blown away that most of the grocery stores carry a variety of maple products (in addition to syrup). There are also sugar houses, which are generally small wooden buildings that maple producers base their operations out of.

For 4-6 weeks (late February-March) the 350+ sugar houses all over the state are busy collecting sap from thawing sugar maples. You can buy sweet treats all year round, but if you visit the sugar houses during maple season you can watch demonstrations of centuries-old craft, enjoy free samples, and possibly go on tours. Some houses offer pancake breakfasts and educational events. This season is a great way to learn about New Hampshire's agriculture and celebrate its natural resources.

# 30. LOBSTER AND CLAM CHOWDER

Few dishes are more New England than "lobstah" and "chowdah." Available in restaurants throughout the state, be sure to sample these at least once during your visit. The best dishes are of course at small local places. One consistently excellent place is Pop's Clam Shell, in Alton Bay. Another is Rye Harbor Lobster Pound, which features a variety of lobster dishes. For lobster rolls, it's important to know the two styles – Connecticut style, served warm with butter, and Maine style, served cold and tossed with mayonnaise. Both are quite satisfying, it just depends on what you're looking for. And few soups will warm you up on a chilly winter day like steaming bowl of clam chowder. I confess, I never liked this soup until I had a homemade batch in New England – it's an entirely different experience from a microwaved can. Whatever seafood you decide to try, know that the people who serve you will be giving you a tasty dish filled with New England pride.

# 31. CRAFT BEER AND BREWERIES

After a long day of exploring the outdoors, sampling food and drink with friends is a satisfying way to wind down. Craft beers are continually gaining in popularity. New Hampshire frequently tops the list as the state with the highest annual consumption of beer, so you know they take it seriously. With over 75 breweries throughout the state, many offering tastings and tours, there's something for beer lovers all over the state. In the White Mountains, Tuckerman's Brewing Company offers daily tours and tastings. Smuttynose Brewing Company, located in Hampton and named for a group of nearby islands, also offers tours and tastings in the southern Seacoast area. Most cities and larger towns have at least one local watering hole to sample craft beers and local favorites. Having lived in the Seacoast area, I can personally recommend Revolution Bar & Grill and Portsmouth Brewing Company. Many of these restaurants carry their love of local craft cuisine into their food as well and offer farm-to-table fare on their menus. Check out Brew NH's website for more detailed ideas.

# 32. ICE CREAM

Dairy farms are an important part of NH's agricultural heritage, and to honor this the Granite State Dairy Promotion sponsors the New Hampshire Ice Cream Trail. You can pick up a passport at NH rest areas and get it stamped at participating locations. Made up of about 50 different sites, you can support family farms throughout the summer by enjoying sweet treats. Many places make their ice cream on site, and/or use only NH made ingredients.

# CULTURAL SITES

# 33. NATURE AND SCIENCE CENTERS

Nature centers are a really fun interactive way to learn about the wildlife that we share a space with. On the Seacoast, you can visit the Great Bay Discovery Center (part of the Great Bay National Estuarine Research Reserve) and learn about estuarine life, as well as interacting with a few animals in the discovery tank. There are interactive displays about research in the bay for adults and children to explore. You can also rent kayaks to paddle around the marshes and experience all the wildlife you just learned about. In the western part of the state, the Harris Center for Conservation Education in Hancock has a great educational center along with over 16 miles of trails in over 35,000 acres of land trust. If you'll be in the area, be sure to check their calendar for events. They sponsor talks from wildlife experts, as well as group hikes and seminars on tracking. In the Lakes Region the Squam Lakes Natural Science Center features a small zoo with local animals, as well as an education center and flower gardens. The animals are all rehabilitated ambassadors for their species. You'll spot wolves, bears, mountain lions, and many other creatures. The live animal exhibit trail is open daily from May 1 through November 1. The science center also hosts a lot of events, such as lake cruises, guided walks, and interpretive talks. These places are especially engaging for young minds, but as an adult I have no trouble enjoying myself!

# 34. WEIRS BEACH

Weirs Beach, or "The Weirs", is a region on the southern shore of Lake Winnipesaukee. The town has existed for centuries, but the sandy beach wasn't actually created until the 1950's. In the present day, the whole area has a delightful atmosphere often found on much bigger seashores. The boardwalk is a great place to stroll, day or night. There is a multitude of eateries and lakefront activities to enjoy. There are also amusement park-esque activities such as go-karting and mini golf. In the summer you'll often happen upon firework shows or live bands performing. Truly, there is something for everyone to enjoy at this lakeside getaway.

# 35. SANTA'S VILLAGE

Are you ever sad that the magic of Christmas is only here for a few weeks in December? Think again and visit Santa's Village in Jefferson, NH. This enchanting amusement park is open May – December. A few attractions, such as Santa's shop and a light show, are open every day the park is. Other events are seasonal. Visit in December to see carolers, reindeer, and the Claus family. There's a

45

New Year's Eve celebration, with a special visit from Santa's reindeer and a spectacular fireworks show. Come in the summer to ride the water rides! During the fall they have foliage rides, and Halloween celebrations. Like many family attractions, this place can be busy during peak weekend and summer days. Visiting in the early summer, or on weekdays during the winter, will give you a chance to tour the place with fewer visitors, but any experience is delightful. Make sure to dress for the weather, and especially don't underestimate the cold. Bundle up in the winter months to maximize your experience!

# 36. CHURCH OF THE WOODS

For many people, nature is sacred. The Church of the Woods, located in the forest of Canterbury, seeks to honor the holiness of all ground and of Mother Earth in an outdoor worship space. An ecumenical church, its worshippers come to feel more in touch with nature and their community. People of all faiths and ages are welcome to visit for their Sunday services (held outside whether it's sunny or snowy) or any other day of the week.

# 37. NH MOTOR SPEEDWAY

The only speedway to host NASCAR National Series events in New England, NH Motor Speedway is located in Loudon, NH and hosts a variety of events year-round. Most famous are the NASCAR races in July, as well as the longest-running motorcycle race in the country, the Loudon Classic. They also host the annual Winston Cup and participate in Bike Week. You can satisfy your personal need for speed by renting out the track for races, or participating in a driving experience yourself. There are also racing schools for cars and motorcycle drivers. In December the speedway hosts the Gift of Lights show, with thousands of Christmas lights on display over the track. It's a great event to get in the holiday spirit.

# 38. HOCKEY GAMES

I've never been a big sports fan, and having been raised farther south, hockey never crossed my mind much as an activity. But no matter who you are, watching a hockey game amongst a spirited crowd of fans is a great experience. The University of New

47

Hampshire's Wildcats hockey games are an excellent opportunity to immerse yourself in a very high-spirited group as hundreds of students chant for their team. The Boston Bruins are the local NHL team, but you can also go watch city club teams compete.

# OUTDOOR ACTIVITIES

## 39. DOG SLED RIDES

For dog-lovers and nature-lovers alike, this is a delightful way in which to experience the outdoors. It's an absolute joy, no matter your age. Flying across the snow in a classic toboggan sled as joyful dogs bark and bound is sure to bring a smile to your face. Generally located in northern NH, teams of sled dogs will be happy to bring you on a journey through New Hampshire's outdoor scenery, as an experienced musher guides the tour. You'll travel through fields and through woods. If you take a ride at night, you might be lucky enough to experience the beauty of winter star-gazing. Tours range from half an hour to just under three hours. Some kennels also offer clinics in which you'll learn a little about mushing yourself and get a chance to drive a team! Many of the dogs are active or retired racers. While this is most often considered a winter activity, some sled dog groups also host tours on wheeled carts during the summer and fall.

# 40. SKI RESORTS & LODGES

When you think New England, you think snow, and skiing is an exhilarating way to enjoy all that snow. Resorts are located throughout the state, and open from December to March, or even April, depending on weather conditions. There are resorts and deals for all skill and age levels. Many resorts will offer discount rental and lift passes for low-volume times (such as late nights and week days). Crotched Mountain, located in Bennington, runs Midnight Madness, allowing you to ski until 3:00 AM! In addition to ski trails most resorts offer activities such as tubing and sledding. Whether you're looking for a week of black diamond trails in the White Mountains or a day-trip with your kids, deals and trails can be found throughout the state.

# 41. CROSS-COUNTRY SKIING AND SNOW-SHOEING

For those that prefer the quiet of the wilderness to the action and bustle of ski mountains, cross-country skiing and snow-shoeing are great ways to enjoy the winter. Cross-country skiing generally goes over flatter terrain. Snow-shoers can really walk wherever there are walking trails. Throughout New Hampshire you can find trails to traverse. Some ski resorts will maintain trails that you need to buy tickets for, but many local parks and woods have trails that are free to access. Depending on what area you go to, you can bring along your dog, either to run alongside or even pull you. Skijoring is the sport of skiing while being pulled by dogs, and a couple places can set you up with a specially made harness. These are good budget winter sports, since rentals of this equipment are generally cheaper than those for downhill skiing. This sport is best enjoyed in the deeper winter months, since you'll need a decent amount of snow cover for your equipment to work well. Ski NH maintains a website with updates of cross-country ski conditions throughout the state.

# 42. SLEIGH RIDES

Sleigh rides seem like the quintessential wintery date, but don't hesitate to ride with your friends too! Throughout New Hampshire you can find farms, inns, or hotels that offer sleigh rides. Some offer an intimate experience with an antique two-person sleigh; others offer rides of up to twenty people at a time. Almost all will provide plenty of blankets, as well as hot cocoa. Whatever the occasion, take a chance to step back in time and experience a slower way of travel. Many of the sleighs are antique or antique style. Rides generally begin in January and end in March, but make sure to check with the individual farm or inn.

# 43. SURFING ON THE SEACOAST

New England might not be a stereotypical hot-spot for surfing, but it's got waves! The waves in the summer tend to be smaller, which makes it a great place for beginners to learn. The northern Atlantic waters are brisk, so this makes a great activity to beat the hot, humid summers. In the fall and winter, the weather picks up and so do the waves. It's cold but

51

it's the best time of year for many die-hard Granite State surfers. Several surf shops along the seacoast (in towns such as Rye and Hampton) will rent out all you need to hit the waves, as well as offering lessons. In addition to a board, you're definitely going to need a wetsuit. Then it's out to the beach! The surf shops I've used are located right across from the waterfront so that you don't have to worry about strapping an enormous foam board to your tiny little compact car. On dry land, you'll first practice paddling and popping up on the beach, and then it's time to practice in the waves. The instructors are really great – if you need it, they'll practically hold your hand, but if all you need is some repetition, they'll stand back and help you gain independence. If it's on your bucket list, I highly encourage you to try it – I've never met anyone who regretted it.

## 44. SCUBA DIVING

This sport is definitely less common in the Granite State, but definitely worth checking out! There are dive shops throughout the state – most, of course, are clustered around the Seacoast, but there are a few in the Lakes Region, and even in a couple near

Manchester, in the center of the state. Almost all the shops offer courses for complete beginners, guided tours, or rentals for those who are already licensed and experienced. There are many lakes in the state that can be fun to dive, and certainly warmer than the ocean. I got my SCUBA certification in the chilly spring ocean waters of New Hampshire, and I'll be the first to admit, it's just plain cold sometimes. But with the right gear, there's plenty to enjoy, including some really awesome marine life and historic remains. Harts Cove, near Fort Constitution in New Castle, is rife with historic artifacts. Dive sites near the Isle of Shoals offer plenty of opportunities for close encounters with the local wildlife. Generally you'll be able to dive between April and October, depending on location. Summer months are warmer, but of course busier. I highly recommend taking the chance to explore a part of NH that most never get to see!

# 45. ROCK CLIMBING

You knew there would have to be something about rocks, in the Granite State, right? There are spots throughout the state (especially for bouldering). One awesome site for sport climbing is at Rumney. The rocks in these routes are actually mostly schist (not granite), which has resulted in a ton of great sport climbing routes. As one of the premier spots for sport climbing in the country, it's very popular with seasoned climbers, but also has plenty of routes for beginners. Though it can sometimes get crowded on popular holidays and weekends, the atmosphere of fellow climbers and the natural scenery itself make this a great spot to visit.

## SPECIAL EVENTS

## 46. BIKE WEEK IN LACONIA

Every year in June, thousands of bikers flock to the Lakes Region to participate in the world's oldest bike rally. In addition to the contests, vendors, and live music, riders can experience some of the most scenic riding in the country. Besides touring on your own, the rally offers group and police escorted rides on certain mountain roads and around Lake Winnipesaukee. It's a great atmosphere, full of energy just as the summer season kicks into full gear.

# 47. CELEBRATE PUMPKINS

Fall is a special time in New Hampshire, and pumpkin festivals are a great way to celebrate it. There are pumpkin games, costume parades, and trick-or-treating. Thousands of jack-o'-lanterns line the streets. How many? In 2013 the city of Keene set a new world record with 30,581 lit jack-o'-lanterns. These events are kid-friendly, but walking through "thousands of smiles" is sure to bring a smile to your face, no matter what your age. The most famous festivals are in Keene and Laconia, but there's also the Milford Pumpkin Festival and the Monadnock Pumpkin Festival.

In addition to pumpkin festivals on land, visit Goffstown in October for their annual Goffstown Pumpkin Weigh Off and Regatta, and watch boaters race gargantuan pumpkins down the Piscataquog River. Grown by New Hampshire's giant pumpkin growers, the pumpkins weigh over 1,000 pounds and are hollowed out and decorated for the race. It's certainly not speed-racing, but it's certainly delightful to watch enormous glittery pumpkins floating down the river, while hundreds of on-lookers cheer. And of course, there's plenty of fair food in the town streets.

# 48. DEERFIELD FAIR

This delightful farm fair takes place in late September in Deerfield, NH. They've got all the typical fair food, and show off anything and everything from New Hampshire's farms. They also have special events each day, such as horse-pulling (an awesome feat of muscle), dog agility competitions, and live performances. There are tractor shows and competitions for the world's largest pumpkin. This event is extremely popular, so the best thing to do is to get tickets in advance and get there early in the day. Parking is located in surrounding fields, so also be sure to mud-proof shoes.

# 49. ICE CASTLES

There are only six places in North America that host ice castles, and Lincoln, NH is one of them. The light and ice displays are absolutely breath-taking. Built to make people smile, the castles are made of thousands of icicles. You'll walk through tunnels, slide down slides, and climb staircases. Take time to simply marvel at the beauty of the sculptures and crystals – you won't be disappointed. There are also occasionally winter princesses that you can see walking around, or special fire shows that really light up the ice.

# 50. WORLD CHAMPIONSHIP SLED DOG DERBY

This is an event dog lovers can't miss. Teams of dogs from all over Canada and the US gather to compete for three days in February in Laconia, NH. Free to watch, dogs and their mushers compete in a variety of races. There are plenty of food vendors, and many of the owners are happy to let you meet their teams of smiling dogs. This event is full of energy and excitement.

# TOP REASONS TO BOOK THIS TRIP

Mountains: Are you just getting started in outdoor sports? Or are you looking for challenging climbs and adventures? No matter – the mountain ranges of New Hampshire have something to challenge and inspire every one of us.

Forests: The most forested state in the Union has un-paralleled opportunities to get up close and personal with our country's natural beauty.

Small Towns: Experience a unique lifestyle throughout New Hampshire's small towns.

History: As one of the original thirteen colonies, many of New Hampshire's towns are older than this country.

BONUS BOOK

# 50 THINGS TO KNOW ABOUT PACKING LIGHT FOR TRAVEL

## PACK THE RIGHT WAY EVERY TIME

AUTHOR: MANIDIPA BHATTACHARYYA

Edited by Melanie Howthorne

# ABOUT THE AUTHOR

Manidipa Bhattacharyya is a creative writer and editor, with an education in English literature and Linguistics. After working in the IT industry for seven long years she decided to call it quits and follow her heart instead. Manidipa has been ghost writing, editing, proof reading and doing secondary research services for many story tellers and article writers for about three years. She stays in Kolkata, India with her husband and a busy two year old. In her own time Manidipa enjoys travelling, photography and writing flash fiction.

Manidipa believes in travelling light and never carries anything that she couldn't haul herself on a trip. However, travelling with her child changed the scenario. She seemed to carry the entire world with her for the baby on the first two trips. But good sense prevailed and she is again working her way to becoming a light traveler, this time with a kid.

# INTRODUCTION

*He who would travel happily*
*must travel light.*

-Antoine de Saint-Exupéry

Travel takes you to different places from seas and mountains to deserts and much more. In your travels you get to interact with different people and their cultures. You will, however, enjoy the sights and interact positively with these new people even more, if you are travelling light.

When you travel light your mind can be free from worry about your belongings. You do not have to spend precious vacation time waiting for your luggage to arrive after a long flight. There is be no chance of your bags going missing and the best part is that you need not pay a fee for checked baggage.

People who have mastered this art of packing light will root for you to take only one carry-on, wherever you go. However, many people can find it really hard to pack light. More so if you are travelling with children. Differentiating between "must have" and "just in case" items is the starting point. There will be ample shopping avenues at your destination which are just waiting to be explored.

This book will show you 'packing' in a new 'light' – pun intended – and help you to embrace light packing practices for all of your future travels.

Off to packing!

## DEDICATION

I dedicate this book to all the travel buffs that I know, who have given me great insights into the contents of their backpacks.

# THE RIGHT TRAVEL GEAR

## 1. CHOOSE YOUR TRAVEL GEAR CAREFULLY

While selecting your travel gear, pick items that are light weight, durable and most importantly, easy to carry. There are cases with wheels so you can drag them along – these are usually on the heavy side because of the trolley. Alternatively a backpack that you can carry comfortably on your back, or even a duffel bag that you can carry easily by hand or sling across your body are also great options. Whatever you choose, one thing to keep in mind is that the luggage itself should not weigh a ton, this will give you the flexibility to bring along one extra pair of shoes if you so desire.

# 2. CARRY THE MINIMUM NUMBER OF BAGS

Selecting light weight luggage is not everything. You need to restrict the number of bags you carry as well. One carry-on size bag is ideal for light travel. Most carriers allow one cabin baggage plus one purse, handbag or camera bag as long as it slides under the seat in front. So technically, you can carry two items of luggage without checking them in.

# 3. PACK ONE EXTRA BAG

Always pack one extra empty bag along with your essential items. This could be a very light weight duffel bag or even a sturdy tote bag which takes up minimal space. In the event that you end up buying a lot of souvenirs, you already have a handy bag to stuff all that into and do not have to spend time hunting for an appropriate bag.

*I'm very strict with my packing and have everything in its right place. I never change a rule. I hardly use anything in the hotel room. I wheel my own wardrobe in and that's it.*

Charlie Watts

# CLOTHES & ACCESSORIES

## 4. PLAN AHEAD

Figure out in advance what you plan to do on your trip. That will help you to pick that one dress you need for the occasion. If you are going to attend a wedding then you have to carry formal wear. If not, you can ditch the gown for something lighter that will be comfortable during long walks or on the beach.

## 5. Wear That Jacket

Remember that wearing items will not add extra luggage for your air travel. So wear that bulky jacket that you plan to carry for your trip. This saves space and can also help keep you warm during the chilly flight.

## 6. MIX AND MATCH

Carry clothes that can be interchangeably used to reinvent your look. Find one top that goes well with a couple of pairs of pants or skirts. Use tops, shirts and jackets wisely along with other accessories like a scarf or a stole to create a new look.

# 7. CHOOSE YOUR FABRIC WISELY

Stuffing clothes in cramped bags definitely takes its toll which results in wrinkles. It is best to carry wrinkle free, synthetic clothes or merino tops. This will eliminate the need for that small iron you usually bring along.

# 8. DITCH CLOTHES PACK UNDERWEAR

Pack more underwear and socks. These are the things that will give you a fresh feel even if you do not get a chance to wear fresh clothes. Moreover these are easy to wash and can be dried inside the hotel room itself.

# 9. CHOOSE DARK OVER LIGHT

While picking your clothes choose dark coloured ones. They are easy to colour coordinate and can last longer before needing a wash. Accidental food spills and dirt from the road are less visible on darker clothes.

# 10. WEAR YOUR JEANS

Take only one pair of Jeans with you, which you should wear on the flight. Remember to pick a pair that can be worn for sightseeing trips and is equally eloquent for dinner. You can add variety by adding light weight cargoes and chinos.

# 11. CARRY SMART ACCESSORIES

The right accessory can give you a fresh look even with the same old dress. An intelligent neck-piece, a couple of bright scarves, stoles or a sarong can be used in a number of ways to add variety to your clothing. These light weight beauties can double up as a nursing cover, a light blanket, beach wear, a modesty cover for visiting places of worship, and also makes for an enthralling game of peek-a-boo.

# 12. LEARN TO FOLD YOUR GARMENTS

Seasoned travellers all swear by rolling their clothes for compact and wrinkle free packing. Bundle packing, where you roll the clothes around a central object as if tying it up, is also a popular method of compact and wrinkle free packing. Stacking folded clothes one on top of another is a big no-no as it makes creases extreme and they are difficult to get rid of without ironing.

# 13. WASH YOUR DIRTY LAUNDRY

One of the ways to avoid carrying loads of clothes is to wash the clothes you carry. At some places you might get to use the laundry services or a Laundromat but if you are in a pinch, best solution is to wash them yourself. If that is the plan then carrying quick drying clothes is highly recommended, which most often also happen to be the wrinkle free variety.

# 14. LEAVE THOSE TOWELS BEHIND

Regular towels take up a lot of space, are heavy and take ages to dry out. If you are staying at hotels they will provide you with towels anyway. If you are travelling to a remote place, where the availability of towels look doubtful, carry a light weight travel towel of viscose material to do the job.

# 15. USE A COMPRESSION BAG

Compression bags are getting lots of recommendation now days from regular travellers. These are useful for saving space in your luggage when you have to pack bulky dresses. While packing for the return trip, get help from the hotel staff to arrange a vacuum cleaner.

# FOOTWEAR

## 16. PUT ON YOUR HIKING BOOTS

If you have plans to go hiking or trekking during your trip, you will need those bulky hiking boots. The best way to carry them is to wear them on flight to save space and luggage weight. You can remove the boots once inside and be comfortable in your socks.

## 17. PICKING THE RIGHT SHOES

Shoes are often the bulkiest items, along with being the dainty if you are a female. They need care and take up a lot of space in your luggage. It is advisable therefore to pick shoes very carefully. If you plan to do a lot of walking and site seeing, then wearing a pair of comfortable walking shoes are a must. For more formal occasions you can carry durable, light weight flats which will not take up much space.

## 18. STUFF SHOES

If you happen to pack a pair of shoes, ensure you utilize their hollow insides. Tuck small items like rolled up socks or belts to save space. They will also be easy to find.

# TOILETRIES

# 19. STASHING TOILETRIES

Carry only absolute necessities. Airline rules dictate that for one carry-on bag, liquids and gels must be in 3.4 ounce (100ml) bottles or less, and must be packed in a one quart zip-lock bag. If you are planning to stay in a hotel, the basic things will be provided for you. It's best is to buy the rest from the local market at your destination.

# 20. TAKE ALONG TAMPONS

Tampons are a hard to find item in a lot of countries. Figure out how many you need and pack accordingly. For longer stays you can buy them online and have them delivered to where you are staying.

# 21. GET PAMPERED BEFORE YOU TRAVEL

Some avid travellers suggest getting a pedicure and manicure just the day before travelling. This not only gives you a well kept look, you also save the trouble of packing nail polish. Remember, every little bit of weight reduced adds up.

# ELECTRONICS

## 22. LUGGING ALONG ELECTRONICS

Electronics have a large role to play in our lives today. Most of us cannot imagine our lives away from our phones, laptops or tablets. However while travelling, one must consider the amount of weight these electronics add to our luggage. Thankfully smart phones come along with all the essentials tools like a camera, email access, picture editing tools and more. They are smart to the point of eliminating the need to carry multiple gadgets. Choose a smart phone that suits all your requirements and travel with the world in your palms or pocket.

## 23. REDUCE THE NUMBER OF CHARGERS

If you do travel with multiple electronic devices, you will have to bear the additional burden of carrying all their chargers too. Check if a single charger can be used for multiple devices. You might also consider investing in a pocket charger. These small devices support multiple devices while keeping you charged on the go.

## 24. TRAVEL FRIENDLY APPS

Along with smart phones come numerous apps, which are immensely helpful in our travels. You name it and you have an app for it at hand – take pictures, sharing with friends and family, torch to light dark roads, maps, checking flight/train times, find hotels and many other things. Use these smart alternatives to traditional items like books to eliminate weight and save space.

*I get ideas about what's essential when packing my suitcase.*

-Diane von Furstenberg

## TRAVELLING WITH KIDS

## 25. BRING ALONG THE STROLLER

Kids might enjoy walking for a while but they soon tire out and a stroller is the just the right thing for them to rest in while you continue your tour. Strollers also double duty as a luggage carrier and shopping bag holder. Remember to pick a light weight, easy to handle brand of stroller. Better yet, find out in advance if you can rent a stroller at your destination.

## 26. BRING ONLY ENOUGH DIAPERS FOR YOUR TRIP

Diapers take up a lot of space and add to the weight of your luggage. Therefore it is advisable to carry just enough diapers to last through the trip and a few for afterwards, till you buy fresh stock at your destination. Unless of course you are travelling to a really remote area, in which case you have no choice but to carry the load. Otherwise diapers are something you will find pretty easily.

## 27. TAKE ONLY A COUPLE OF TOYS

Children are easily attracted by new things in their environment. While travelling they will find numerous 'new' objects to scrutinize and play with. Packing just one favorite toy is enough, or if there is no favorite toy leave out all of them in favor of stories or imaginary games.

## 28. CARRY KID FRIENDLY SNACKS

Create a small snack counter in your bag to store away quick bites for those sudden hunger pangs. Depending on the child's age this could include chocolates, raisins, dry fruits, granola bars or biscuits. Also keep a bottle of water handy for your little one.

These things do not add much weight and can be adjusted in a handbag or knapsack.

# 29. GAMES TO CARRY

Create some travel specific, imaginary games if you have slightly grown up children, like spot the attractions. Keep a coloring book and colors handy for in-flight or hotel time. Apps on your smart phone can keep the children engaged with cartoons and story books. Older children are often entertained by games available on phones or tablets. This cuts the weight of luggage down while keeping the kids entertained.

# 30. LET THE KIDS CARRY THEIR LOAD

A good thing is to start early sharing of responsibilities. Let your child pick a bag of his or her choice and pack it themselves. Keep tabs on what they are stuffing in their bags by asking if they will be using that item on the trip. It could start out being just an entertainment bag initially but with growing years they will learn to sort the useful from the superfluous. Children as little as four can maneuver a small trolley suitcase like a pro- their experience in pull along toys credit. If you are worried that you may be pulling it for them, you may want to start with a backpack.

## 31. DECIDE ON LOCATION FOR CHILDREN TO SLEEP

While on a trip you might not always get a crib at your destination, and carrying one will make life all the more difficult. Instead call ahead to see if there are any cribs or roll out beds for children. You may even put blankets on the floor. Weave them a story about camping and they will gladly sleep without any trouble.

## 32. GET BABY PRODUCTS DELIVERED AT YOUR DESTINATION

If you are absolutely paranoid about not getting your favourite variety of diaper or brand of baby food, check out online stores like amazon.com for services in your destination city. You can buy things online ahead of your travel and get them delivered to your hotel upon arrival.

## 33. FEEDING NEEDS OF YOUR INFANTS

If you are travelling with a breastfed infant, you save the trouble of carrying bottles and bottle sanitization kits. For special food, or medications, you may need to call ahead to make sure you have a refrigerator where you are staying.

# 34. FEEDING NEEDS OF YOUR TODDLER

With the progression from infancy to toddler, their dietary requirements too evolve. You will have to pack some snacks for travelling time. Fresh fruits and vegetables can be purchased at your destination. Most of the cities you travel to in whichever part of the world, will have baby food products and formulas, available at the local drug-store or the supermarket.

# 35. PICKING CLOTHES FOR YOUR BABY

Contrary to popular belief, babies can do without many changes of clothes. At the most pack 2 outfits per day. Pack mix and match type clothes for your little one as well. Pick things which are comfortable to wear and quick to dry.

# 36. SELECTING SHOES FOR YOUR BABY

Like outfits, kids can make do with two pairs of comfortable shoes. If you can get some water resistant shoes it will be best. To expedite drying wet shoes, you can stuff newspaper in them then wrap them with newspaper and leave them to dry overnight.

## 37. KEEP ONE CHANGE OF CLOTHES HANDY

Travelling with kids can be tricky. Keep a change of clothes for the kids and mum handy in your purse or tote bag. This takes a bit of space in your hand luggage but comes extremely handy in case there are any accidents or spills.

## 38. LEAVE BEHIND BABY ACCESSORIES

Baby accessories like their bed, bath tub, car seat, crib etc. should be left at home. Many hotels provide a crib on request, while car seats can be borrowed from friends or rented. Babies can be given a bath in the hotel sink or even in the adult bath tub with a little bit of water. If you bring a few bath toys, they can be used in the bath, pool, and out of water. They can also be sanitized easily in the sink.

## 39. CARRY A SMALL LOAD OF PLASTIC BAGS

With children around there are chances of a number of soiled clothes and diapers. These plastic bags help to sort the dirt from the clean inside your big bag. These are very light weight and come in handy to other carry stuff as well at times.

# PACK WITH A PURPOSE

## 40. PACKING FOR BUSINESS TRIPS

One neutral-colored suit should suffice. It can be paired with different shirts, ties and accessories for different occasions. One pair of black suit pants could be worn with a matching jacket for the office or with a snazzy top for dinner.

## 41. PACKING FOR A CRUISE

Most cruises have formal dinners, and that formal dress usually takes up a lot of space. However you might find a tuxedo to rent. For women, a short black dress with multiple accessory options will do the trick.

## 42. PACKING FOR A LONG TRIP OVER DIFFERENT CLIMATES

The secret packing mantra for travel over multiple climates is layering. Layering traps air around your body creating insulation against the cold. The same light t-shirt that is comfortable in a warmer climate can be the innermost layer in a colder climate.

# REDUCE SOME MORE WEIGHT

## 43. LEAVE PRECIOUS THINGS AT HOME

Things that you would hate to lose or get damaged leave them at home. Precious jewelry, expensive gadgets or dresses, could be anything. You will not require these on your trip. Leave them at home and spare the load on your mind.

## 44. SEND SOUVENIRS BY MAIL

If you have spent all your money on purchasing souvenirs, carrying them back in the same bag that you brought along would be difficult. Either pack everything in another bag and check it in the airport or get everything shipped to your home. Use an international carrier for a secure transit, but this could be more expensive than the checking fees at the airport.

## 45. AVOID CARRYING BOOKS

Books equal to weight. There are many reading apps which you can download on your smart phone or tab. Plus there are gadgets like Kindle and Nook that are thinner and lighter alternatives to your regular book.

# CHECK, GET, SET, CHECK AGAIN

## 46. STRATEGIZE BEFORE PACKING

Create a travel list and prepare all that you think you need to carry along. Keep everything on your bed or floor before packing and then think through once again – do I really need that? Any item that meets this question can be avoided. Remove whatever you don't really need and pack the rest.

## 47. TEST YOUR LUGGAGE

Once you have fully packed for the trip take a test trip with your luggage. Take your bags and go to town for window shopping for an hour. If you enjoy your hour long trip it is good to go, if not, go home and reduce the load some more. Repeat this test till you hit the right weight.

## 48. ADD A ROLL OF DUCT TAPE

You might wonder why, when this book has been talking about reducing stuff, we're suddenly asking you to pack something totally unusual. This is because when you have limited supplies, duct tape is immensely helpful for small repairs – a broken bag, leaking zip-lock bag, broken sunglasses, you name it and duct tape can fix it, temporarily.

# 49. LIST OF ESSENTIAL ITEMS

Even though the emphasis is on packing light, there are things which have to be carried for any trip. Here is our list of essentials:

•Passport/Visa or any other ID

•Any other paper work that might be required on a trip like permits, hotel reservation confirmations etc.

•Medicines – all your prescription medicines and emergency kit, especially if you are travelling with children

•Medical or vaccination records

•Money in foreign currency if travelling to a different country

•Tickets- Email or Message them to your phone

# 50. MAKE THE MOST OF YOUR TRIP

Wherever you are going, whatever you hope to do we encourage you to embrace it whole-heartedly. Take in the scenery, the culture and above all, enjoy your time away from home.

*On a long journey even a straw weighs heavy.*

-Spanish Proverb

# PACKING AND PLANNING TIPS

## A Week before Leaving

- Arrange for someone to take care of pets and water plants.

- Stop mail and newspaper.

- Notify Credit Card companies where you are going.

- Change your thermostat settings.

- Car inspected, oil is changed, and tires have the correct pressure.

- Passports and photo identification is up to date.

- Pay bills.

- Copy important items and download travel Apps.

- Start collecting small bills for tips.

## Right Before Leaving

- Clean out refrigerator.

- Empty garbage cans.

- Lock windows.

- Make sure you have the proper identification with you.

- Bring cash for tips.

- Remember travel documents.

- Lock door behind you.

- Remember wallet.

- Unplug items in house and pack chargers.

# READ OTHER
# GREATER THAN A TOURIST
# BOOKS

Greater Than a Tourist San Miguel de Allende Guanajuato Mexico:
50 Travel Tips from a Local by Tom Peterson

Greater Than a Tourist – Lake George Area New York USA:
 50 Travel Tips from a Local by Janine Hirschklau

Greater Than a Tourist – Monterey California United States:
50 Travel Tips from a Local by Katie Begley

 Greater Than a Tourist – Chanai Crete Greece:
50 Travel Tips from a Local by Dimitra Papagrigoraki

Greater Than a Tourist – The Garden Route Western Cape Province
South Africa:  50 Travel Tips from a Local by Li-Anne McGregor van
Aardt

Greater Than a Tourist – Sevilla Andalusia Spain:
50 Travel Tips from a Local by Gabi Gazon

Greater Than a Tourist – Kota Bharu Kelantan Malaysia:
50 Travel Tips from a Local by Aditi Shukla

Children's Book: Charlie the Cavalier Travels the World by Lisa
Rusczyk

>TOURIST

Visit Greater Than a Tourist for Free Travel Tips
http://GreaterThanATourist.com

Sign up for the Greater Than a Tourist Newsletter for discount days, new books, and travel information:
http://eepurl.com/cxspyf

Follow us on Facebook for tips, images, and ideas:
https://www.facebook.com/GreaterThanATourist

Follow us on Pinterest for travel tips and ideas:
http://pinterest.com/GreaterThanATourist

Follow us on Instagram for beautiful travel images:
http://Instagram.com/GreaterThanATourist

>TOURIST

At Greater Than a Tourist, we love to share travel tips with you. How did we do? What guidance do you have for how we can give you better advice for your next trip? Please send your feedback to GreaterThanaTourist@gmail.com as we continue to improve the series. We appreciate your constructive feedback. Thank you.

>TOURIST

# METRIC CONVERSIONS

## TEMPERATURE

110° F —      — 40° C
100° F —
90° F —       — 30° C
80° F —
70° F —       — 20° C
60° F —
50° F —       — 10° C
40° F —
32° F —       — 0° C
20° F —
10° F —       — -10° C
0° F —         — -18° C
-10° F —
-20° F —      — -30° C

### To convert F to C:

Subtract 32, and then multiply by 5/9 or .5555.

### To Convert C to F:

Multiply by 1.8 and then add 32.

### 32F = 0C

## LIQUID VOLUME

To Convert:...................Multiply by
U.S. Gallons to Liters................ 3.8
U.S. Liters to Gallons ................26
Imperial Gallons to U.S. Gallons 1.2
Imperial Gallons to Liters....... 4.55
Liters to Imperial Gallons ........22
**1 Liter = .26 U.S. Gallon**
**1 U.S. Gallon = 3.8 Liters**

## DISTANCE

To convert .............Multiply by
Inches to Centimeters ....2.54
Centimeters to Inches ........39
Feet to Meters...................... .3
Meters to Feet ...................3.28
Yards to Meters ..................91
Meters to Yards ................1.09
Miles to Kilometers ..........1.61
Kilometers to Miles............ .62
**1 Mile = 1.6 km**
**1 km = .62 Miles**

## WEIGHT

1 Ounce = .28 Grams
1 Pound = .4555 Kilograms
1 Gram = .04 Ounce
1 Kilogram = 2.2 Pounds

93

# TRAVEL QUESTIONS

- Do you bring presents home to family or friends after a vacation?

- Do you get motion sick?

- Do you have a favorite billboard?

- Do you know what to do if there is a flat tire?

- Do you like a sun roof open?

- Do you like to eat in the car?

- Do you like to wear sun glasses in the car?

- Do you like toppings on your ice cream?

- Do you use public bathrooms?

- Did you bring your cell phone and does it have power?

- Do you have a form of identification with you?

- Have you ever been pulled over by a cop?

- Have you ever given money to a stranger on a road trip?

- Have you ever taken a road trip with animals?

- Have you ever went on a vacation alone?

- Have you ever run out of gas?

- If you could move to any place in the world, where would it be?

- If you could travel anywhere in the world, where would you travel?

- If you could travel in any vehicle, which one would it be?

- If you had three things to wish for from a magic genie, what would they be?

- If you have a driver's license, how many times did it take you to pass the test?

- What are you the most afraid of on vacation?

- What do you want to get away from the most when you are on vacation?

- What foods smells bad to you?

- What item do you bring on ever trip with you away from home?

- What makes you sleepy?

- What song would you love to hear on the radio when you're cruising on the highway?

- What travel job would you want the least?

- What will you miss most while you are away from home?

- What is something you always wanted to try?

- What is the best road side attraction that you ever saw?

- What is the farthest distance you ever biked?

- What is the farthest distance you ever walked?

- What is the weirdest thing you needed to buy while on vacation?

- What is your favorite candy?

- What is your favorite color car?

- What is your favorite family vacation?

- What is your favorite food?

- What is your favorite gas station drink or food?

- What is your favorite license plate design?

- What is your favorite restaurant?

- What is your favorite smell?

- What is your favorite song?

- What is your favorite sound that nature makes?

- What is your favorite thing to bring home from a vacation?

- What is your favorite vacation with friends?

- What is your favorite way to relax?

- Where is the farthest place you ever traveled in a car?

- Where is the farthest place you ever went North, South, East and West?

- Where is your favorite place in the world?

- Who is your favorite singer?

- Who taught you how to drive?

- Who will you miss the most while you are away?

- Who if the first person you will contact when you get to your destination?

- Who brought you on your first vacation?

- Who likes to travel the most in your life?

- Would you rather be hot or cold?

- Would you rather drive above, below, or at the speed limited?

- Would you rather drive on a highway or a back road?

- Would you rather go on a train or a boat?

- Would you rather go to the beach or the woods?

# TRAVEL BUCKET LIST

1.

2.

3.

4.

5.

6.

7.

8.

9.

10.

# NOTES

Made in the USA
Monee, IL
17 March 2021